HOLD THAT THOUGHT

ISBN: 9798837998928



Cover art - “Reverberations”, Kathleen Moser, 1981

Acknowledgements:

Gift - *The Brockport Forum*

## Contents

# ALCOHOL

Rum
colors the ice rich
tints a wedge of lime,
swirls over the lumpy esophagus,
drizzles into the stomach,
bubbles there with acid
and food sludge,
spirals out into coils
of glistening intestine,
twists among the capillaries,
sneaks across vessel walls,
rushes through plasma
at expressway speeds, leukocytes
and red cells merging merging,
so much metabolic traffic,
exit ramps to the brain,
where all the cooked up neurons
still raging in their bone cage,
sop enough alcohol
to flare, clean blue flame
after clean blue flame,
to the soothing,
blissful
hum.

## DONATION

On my finger tip an agitated crowd assembles
to a globule and drops
into a beaker, dark
tarry settling blood,
the correct red concentration
that can be taken.

Questions about sex with whom, sex
how often, sex and age, exposures
to this, afflictions
with any of listed conditions,
journeys, pregnancies, surgeries,
all noted.  I lie down.

My arm is tied with a rubber strip,
painted betadine orange, tapped
like an autumn maple.
I squeeze the ball, slowly
at first, steadily, harder
to pump the full measure.

I don't escape easily.
I am offered juice, sip cola,
am I lightheaded? There is
an assortment of cookies,
a small red badge,
"kiss me, I gave blood."

Kiss me, I am a tributary, pouring
into the throb and flow
that must never dry away
to nothing left, nothing
to brush a blush

across a pale cheek.

## STROKE

It is even before its world is bone,
during the forming, before
time draws breath,
that all blood movement begins.
Every cell, red or white,
starts motion. Pale fighters,
red nurturers, in this busy process
demanding relentless circulation.

They push and rush
along slippery thoroughfares,
tumbling over and under
in the currents. They gather
at places of injury or pain.
Some are lost in daily small
bleedings, others to cycles
of potentials washed away.

They race their highways,
veer onto ramps and routes
to every destination, to broad
back muscle, dreaming cranial neurons,
lungs giving breathing to songs,
eardrums that receive songs,
sobs or thunder. Some cells shiver
with suspicion that behind all of it
is a tireless heart.

But the aging of its bone world
causes the progress of blood
to grow sluggish and thick.
Passages narrow. There is
crowding until one moment

becomes too small
to negotiate a turning. Chaos
at the bottleneck and a corner
closes.

## RINGING

Inside my bell,
within this metal shape,
the shape of validity,
how they measure curves,
air contains itself.
The quiet is equal
only
to immobility.

Inside any bell
there is only one
thing to be, a clapper.
I don't mean
to give applause,
I mean to bang
my tempered soul
against the hard walls
of definition.

It's my collisions
inside my bell,
my impact
that makes the air
of my world ring.
I think I pull the ropes or
maybe something larger
pulls the ropes,

creates my swings
of pain, resonates
my air, anticipates
bell tones,
I can't stop

ringing.

## THE HORIZON PENETRATED BY PURPLE

On these mornings when
the horizon is penetrated by purple,
hills melt into hills into forever,
in an impressionism too much
to fit through my eyes
all the way back into meanings.
Mornings without time
that begin untethered
are to be lost in,
to drift into until substance
is bequeathed to whatever is left
behind. If I return
to the sum of things,
where everything is held
by nothing, I can travel mists
to places that are not
places, dimensionless,
places to be without being,
like anesthesia before sleep,
I will not feel,
I will be without,
in a realm where
absences are
and presences are not,
through grays
to green-blacks to
such violet
vacuum.

## BORROWING THE TIMES

What could the old man be thinking
after I startle him from worn tweed thoughts,
asking, *are you through with the Times?*

He blinks, his mind hurrying around
to tidy up for this unexpected visitor.
*It's my Times, I paid for it!* His eyes surprised.
Like cartoon balloons, confusion punctuates
both our faces.

*I'm so sorry, I thought it was a library copy.*
*I thought you had finished reading. My mistake.*
As he understands, he smiles, like the gallant young man
he must have always been. *Oh, I see. Yes, certainly.*
*I'm through reading. Here, take it please.*

*Oh, I couldn't, I thought it was a library copy...*
but he insists softly, *It's my pleasure. Take it please.*
I take the paper and the echo of my thank you
a distance of three chairs away. His New York Times,
thick, complex, like the city it serves, the city
where one time I had to buy a postcard of a photograph
entitled "Lost Cloud" just because of the image.

I watch the back of his worn tweed jacket, spun white hair
as he stares through the windows for a time. Outside
the city goes by at various speeds. He's becoming the cloud
in my post card, suspended and alone, amidst the soaring
and glorious geometry of skyscrapers no longer there

in his city, our city. I imagine rain
separated from the rest of the storm,
and the winds that must
have carried it.

## SAME OLD WOMAN

Her face
is as if she means to learn,
she moves her body strictly
and carries parcels.
I wouldn't need to care but
she reappears
everywhere,
there along Huckleberry Road,
walking toward a bus stop,
isn't it that same old woman there
on a Seventh Street sidewalk,
see the parcels
see the sternness, and
from inside the laundromat I see
her cross the picture window,
pushing parcels and purpose.
I think how strange, and then again
in St. Luke's Hospital she's there
serious and still
near the crowded elevator,
unreal as this has to be,
there she is in the parking lot,
parcels and angular purpose
from empty spot to empty spot,
and now, along the chain link fence
surrounding Hillside cemetery,
stern, unwavering, parcels and pace,
and now within my rearview mirror,
is it finally that she fades
behind my anxious acceleration?

## THE FIRST DAWN SHE WILL NOT SEE

stirs crimson at the horizon,
just an hour after the phone call,
a day after I brushed her hair back
from her forehead to whisper
*you'll be an angel soon, Mom,*
as she worked for every breath
and her eldest son asked
*are we sure she can't get stronger,*
his eyes filling at the hospice nurse reply,
*you feel like the little boy again,*
*who doesn't want his mother to leave,*
as all of us who love her so,
now must learn to let her go.

# TEMPER

My creature snarls,
snaps at the air,
nothing to do about it,
it's the breed, aggressive,
deep inside its marrow.
Hackles raised, lips curled,
all teeth, growling low
inside its throat, ears flat
against its skull, it sees
only threat and
when it lunges,
it will be for the throat.

## AUTOPSY

Case #11911 Autopsy# 03A-6669
Name - Grace Madden. Age - 72 Race - W. Sex - F
Attending Physicians - The doctors and doctors
Time and date of death - so soon
Permission granted for this autopsy - spouse
Reason for autopsy - to know why

*We would know why, someone would analyze,*
*grandchildren would realize Grandma is dead.*

Gross anatomical description - Scars of lateral chest wall due to past surgery.
Recent healing chest wound, secondary to pneumonectomy. Multiple rib fractures,
secondary to CPR procedures.
*They tried. Medics, emergency room personnel pushed*
*and pressed on Grandma's heart. But it remained still.*

Chronic myocarditis, changes attributable to viral and other microscopic agents.
Enlargement of heart. Evidence of residual tumor in left lung.

*Other lives settled in Grandma's large heart.*
*Other lives crowded her breathing.*

Anatomical external description - Body of elderly white female with thinning
white hair. Remainder of head and neck areas are unremarkable.

*Her hair when she was Grandpa's new bride was a brushed flame,*
*passed as a crown to her granddaughter. Grandma had a remarkable smile.*

A recent incisional chest wound and well healed scar from previous surgery.

*Grandma told us how a body grows past its pain, how a soul knits*
*its own scars and now, she is somewhere else.*

Right hand, fourth finger contains a silver ring with an amethyst stone and the fourth
finger of the left hand contains a small diamond ring and gold wedding band.

*She cried her smiles on her fiftieth birthday,*
*such a smoky purple! as Grandpa kissed her cheek.*

Clinical history, 72-year-old white female, recently discharged from St. Bridget's following a pneumonectomy for carcinoma of the left lung. Family stated patient had a "good night" but following morning felt faint at breakfast. EMS crew initiated CPR at patient's home, continued by emergency room staff upon arrival at hospital at 10:37AM. Patient was declared dead at 11:19AM.

*Cause of death - surprise, secondary to shock of life not seeming finished.*
*Grandma's eyes widened. Smells of bacon and coffee, steam from the waffle maker,*
*continued to float in the citric morning sunlight and nothing else*
*stopped, even after she gasped and nodded her head.*

## STRINGS

In the rococo symphony hall
it's not the strings, not
the tentative piano,
it's huddling memories pulled
from hiding that cry or need
so much to cry.

One chair holds Daniel.
He walks on the music
back to a high school corridor,
alone, hands huddled in tuxedo pockets
while each wall sings back to him
songs of his only senior prom,
his only girl, how she finds him

pressing his forehead against
his dented locker door, he turns
and when she touches his cheek,
he pulls hard away, runs
down long empty halls
once crowded with friends and dreams,
she cries, surrounded by dark geometric
echoes of the last prom song, his fading steps,

her eyes just like the eyes
in the rococo symphony hall,
as people blink and remark how music
makes them cry, almost cry, but
it's not the strings, it's empty hallways
through songs of something ending,
footsteps echoing away.

## THE MIGRAINE

Inside
there is pain
kicking like mustangs
against the bone of my skull,
so I try to run fast enough,
hard enough, until
breathing hurts,
because if I push
until muscles burn
and the cinder running path
begins to blur, then
my throbbing head
may finally
become a carousel,
pain prancing away in sparkles
while my throbs only
carnival music around the red,
black, yellow, blue, even
palomino painted steeds
in their galloping shining,
and then

I would be able to ride
their magical stampede,
all the way inside
to a black and gentle
spindle.

# THE ILLUSTRATION

With her curious silence,
she stands very still in my calendar.
She could be me in our back yard
beneath grape vines, frozen
in one twelfth of 1956.

She is turning toward the feeling
of my eyes, something her ears
might see, but couldn't understand
how I watch her in water color, held
on the page called August, but

she is fictional, like my past,
and can't remember taking
a woman's steps beneath hemlock
brushing her forehead, stopping
just that moment on the trail

to look back, while others
laughed and hiked ahead.
I can name a child in a calendar
any name, she is the one behind
prophesies and trees, the one

in wet sunlight, named me, but
still she stays in August 2015,
always looking, always
on this page, on a cycle, on the skin
of a bursting fragrant grape.

# BREATH TAKING VALLEY

Seeing her finally, haunted Donegal eyes,
I say how glad I am to meet her,
Kathy's birth mother, Mary Rose
and I hug her, feeling how real she is.
She replies, *You're Kathleen's friend,*
*all her life, aren't you? Well yes,*
*since third grade, Catholic school.*
*How lovely!* She takes the flowers
I bought in Ardara. *Come inside, please.*

Inside the white farm house, under
the thatch roof, a house nestled
against the mountain in Glengesh Pass,
a view that "takes your breath" even
if all your life you've lived
within its mythic spell. All of us
are ushered to the sitting room.
Without enough chairs there is confusion,
shuffling, polite debates about seating

until everyone is settled and stepfather John Francis
asks *will we be having a wee nip?* Of course
we will and fine Irish whiskey is poured,
served on the painted tin tray. Kathy's brother
beams a handsome Irish grin, extending his hand.
*This is Phillip,* explains Mary Rose, *Beth, his wife,*
*and this is Sharon, John Damien's wife.*
*They've just built that lovely home near the road.*

A large, peat-fueled stove sits in the hearth.
It warms the home and makes the meals.
Mary Rose shows me the blocks of turf, then
adds one to the pieces of combustible Ireland

already burning. We chat, waiting on the kettle,
as sweet nut breads, baked just this morning
are served. There are questions about Pennsylvania,
about Donegal, stories of our journey, the pubs,
the three Welshmen, here for a rugby tournament,
who bought us too many pints in Galway,
the narrow Irish roads, driving on the left, and

Glengesh Pass... *Surely, it always still*
*takes my breath away!* Phillip exclaims,
and how Kathleen has Mary Rose's eyes.
John Francis talks of prejudice, religions,
different peoples and how they are all really
the same. And me, am I Irish too? *A bit.*
*My father is half Irish, half, Welsh, all Celt*
*though.* I chuckle. *My mother is French.*
*The Welshmen in Galway said the Welsh*
*don't really like the French.* John Francis
insists the French are fine and his eyes shine
at Mary Rose, their new daughter, his family
getting to know her and her friends. *This farmhouse*
he announces, *has been in my family*
*nearly 200 years!* Then he adds,

as if it just occurs to him, *You'll be needing*
*to be off to Carrigart before dark. Kathleen's*
*sister will be expecting you.* I can't say anything
that seems enough to Mary Rose, as she poses
for just another photo, standing self-conscious
but smiling with her eyes still shell-shocked
from half a century ago when pious nuns
in Roscrea took this child from her.
Surrounded by her now complete family
she stands, the incarnate dream of 8-year-olds
who in a school yard a lifetime ago, wondered
where she was, who she was, almost knowing

of a breath-taking valley in Donegal,
an ocean away from their parochial school,
and a young mother who held her fair-haired toddler,
that she had named, nursed and, when ordered to,
dressed her in her finest purple coat, and then
screamed as they took her away.

# GIFT

The boy with sparkling giggle eyes
held out his hand cups
glistening with orange glass chips
of candy, he offered with a grin.

Not just candy, I tasted
electricity flavored orange,
crackling static sugar on my tongue.
I ran amazed to tell the others.

# IRIS

Unquestionably
the iris wears its silks
like a lady, and flags
her femininity unabashed
in dazzling afternoon light.
In the crowded bed
she stands tall on her stem
with grace and conviction
in the intrinsic truth
that blooming
is the meaning, purpose
and destiny
of being alive.

# THE BROOK

as it bubbles
sounds so consistent
I could dismiss it, but
some of it bubbles incisively
with opinion and argument,
tumbling air over itself and under,
until the journey over rocks
is accomplished
in a splash and clarity
and determination to flow.

## DAIQUIRI

Current turning the blades
and apricots growl themselves
into nectar,
with run sugar ice,
we think it's nice
this drink for gods, we feel
our divinity
over summer, over our weathered dock,
freshly pale green
in weather resistant paint.

Draped over the edge, full
of rum and liquified apricots,
I watch my reflection float itself,
pieces ripple off and rush away.
I wonder why I stare so
analytical, so pale and intense,
when my wavy face holds
no rigid edge, like
a lake without a shore.

Lakes have nestled in the pits of land,
longer than families have flared
down their generations.
I boldly toast this lake,
this earth-colored jewel
that flashes back the sun,
its surface swirled by wakes of boats,
arcing forever melting patterns that
ripple and rush to shore,
blades turning the current.

# GYPSY MOTH

The girl before the fire
has eyes like embers, and
and behind their heat,
the strings and tambourines
ignite a musical yearning, reach
for secret flames, for the red
relentless one inside her breast.
A blush singes her forehead, flares
along her face until she pulls lace
down off her shoulders. Burning
summer nights seduce her, she dreams
to leave the painted wagons.

She wants to stamp her feet
beside thunder, clasp
a lightening bolt to her chest,
raise her skirts and kick
the helmet from a cossack,
or with a softest flick
of her fingers, brush hair away
from the stormy eyes of a priest.
She slaps her tambourine
against her thighs, whirls
and whirls, in red and yellow
satin swirls around,
around the fire.

## THE WEDDING POEM

Last night, noisy crickets
suggested gifts for the wedding pair.
Offer them wheat light
from an August field,
October's warm implications
fallen orange and gold,
offer them moon gilded snow
on their first Christmas Eve,
offer them this September day.

They walked the distance of a blush
to this moment made for them and
because we are friends,
we walked along, from time to time.
Today, under morning glory vines
we celebrate and witness,
and we offer the shine
of all unfurling stars
to Kathy and to Paul,

a similar eye shine in all of us.
Bless them, bless all that love them,
bless their love as it opens
blue to the skies,
bless their faith
petal by petal,
as it kisses the brow
of every morning that blushes
across the rest of their lives.

## ADMITTED

Padding around on strange slippers,
around corridors, around corners,
clasping arms around myself
to contain shaking,
prevent explosion
onto sanitary walls.

They all know I'm here,
my existence too loud,
wailing into spaces
between stares. Pad and pad,
deafening flap, strange blue slippers,
not mine, peeking to turn a corner,
avoid threat of approach. They
are trained, can read my bracelet.

Pad around to tap it off,
the pushing inside, strains
against all efforts. Corridors
stretch narrower, corners
become obtuse. My existence
is too loud, can't control volume,
couldn't possibly be being
this much.

Slippers shuffling faster,
slapping sloppy panic,
my room, what
was the number,
all these people
in the way.

I squeeze my arms tighter,

try to smile, shouldn’t
have left my room, what if
someone else is in it
now, what if I have no place,
even here?

## IN THE "MENTAL" HOSPITAL

every face is a hurricane's eye, every
eye swollen by pain that flows
or tries to, and I tell myself
the storm inside my soul
is what brings this April snow,
and one day later,
causes a cyclone
that lifts a garage roof
from the last house in the row,
and so, I know
I must be in Oz
and there has to be
a wizard.

## EXPLANATION
("...there was no suicide note...")

Inside my head
such wind,
nothing but wind,
whirling,
excruciating orbits
of everything,
so much wind,
stones under my feet,
useless crying,
nothing but wind,
walking fast,
almost running
away from wind,
on a gravel road
melting into black,
nothing but black,
drawn to the black
like a child's hand to fire,
drawn to the black blanket,
black pond, deep enough
to drift beneath, quiet
under the black, no wind,
slapping breath from my face,
no more wind, just
blessed black, this blessed
black embrace.

## WOMAN TAKES HER OWN LIFE

This headline
freezing tides
with its silent sentence.
In the parlor,
blankets of mums
cover everything unspoken,
coalesced into funeral.

When she was still
a whirlpool,
an ocean of being
around a vortex of bone,
landlocked by form,
she used to think in streams
of flowing beyond.

Her whirling,
her gyroscope mind
was deceptively still.
Her spinning unwound itself
into hemorrhage,
from her center,
her bony remains.

## NAME SOUND

When he enters the sunny bedroom
and moves closer to her,
sees no breathing,
feels no warmth,
a scream explodes
from a place in his chest,
a molten scream pours
from his throat,
forms itself into her name
and empties him.

Her name
escapes his crumbling body,
flees out into the street,
climbs the skies. It goes
forever, past
ears, past atmosphere,
out,
a sound of nothing
in nothing.

## WRITERS' CONFERENCE (SQUAW VALLEY)

To walk away enough is hard.
An hour drive to Reno,
three jets, three takeoffs,
piecing a journey by thirds
to the other side of America.
I assemble faces behind jet lag,
till they seep around my eyes,
and close my throat,
friends that will not be held
or easily found again.

Thursday evening we rode the tram
down from High Camp
and there was speculation
in the crowded car.
If the cable broke,
a containment of songs
would plunge to a low note,
rupture open against rock
and pour poetry everywhere.

We curved our mouths around the if
as if comedy were the point,
giggling at the idea of tragedy
because stepping the days
through a Squaw Valley week
had made everything a metaphor,
how could there ever be endings
or walking away?

## UNSUMMONED

I feel you,
dark cold purple.
Your red talons work wretchedly
with greed. They brand
whatever they touch.
Your lips smack loudly
between hissing breaths, sour breaths.

The nearer you com,
larger,
I shrink from the wrongness of you
and you solidify.

You must leave.
I ask it with life in my mind,
white birches, evergreens in snow,
a baby's smell, a rose,
tracing the ear of love.

I command you to leave
with prayer,
with an angel's hand on my shoulder

and now you leave,
the room only a room again.
Winter midnight shines
through the long window.
I am safe
within a curl of sleep.

# BUTTERFLY PLACE

Close to the edge of the road
30 or 40 white wedges of silk
assemble on macadam, and
when I drive by
they fly into air,
hovering insect flowers,
or collected souls of 37 deer
killed last November, maybe,
but still why at this one place,
about one square foot in the stones
on Blacksmith Road.

A butterfly place, I think
and look to sky, to white lines
in the road
for agreement, look to the broken oak
for some answer.

Twenty minutes later,
coming back home,
I pass them,
still assembled until
my car rolls near enough
and they rise
in such commotion,
and land again on that same
butterfly place. I have no choice
but to drive home
with all my questions.

## ORACLE

Feeling the bite of each breath,
each step over the wooden bridge,
I cross the small river, running hard,
pushing space before me
as if air were a heavy thing.
She waits for these times,
regal dusks, horizons
of purple flame, *I'm here,*
she whispers, *What do you need to know?*
Her voice is always in wind
rushing by my ears, my questions
always in the rhythm of the run,
*Know that secrets in the moon are revealed*

*in the waxing and waning of selves.*
*Pay tender attention to snow,*
*to cardinals, the breath of pines.*
*Notice the thin fingers of willows*
*pointing to earth, to promises*
*beneath silver grasses, to promises*
*of seasons.* I follow her gestures,
attenuated reaches; her eyes are silver.
*There are those,* she murmurs,
*made to come out of night,* and fainter,
*out of a cyclical light,*
and fainter still, *made*
*to contain tides.* I don't hear
her leaving, don't feel the moment
pour away.

## FORMS OF WATER

So much of it
is not just trees, all these trees
next to streams or a lake
or pool where I watch,
I love to watch.
A heavy woman, face puckered
like her thighs, with excess
and bewilderment and dreams
she buried in flesh, or a soft mother,
haloed with a weight of hair, her baby lady
on her hip, posed like happiness
near the concrete steps.

Red pigtails fly by the diving boards
while a lifeguard uses his tan and whistle
with salaried care. White water boys sizzle
toward the energy of hard-muscled men,
a grandfather's grey chest softens down
into time and the pool edge, he loses
power to finally gain it. Waves
take their turns into shore,
into shore, they are all the same,
they always change.

Lakes and pools surround without comment.
I stare at stripes of waves, again and again
to the banks, in speeds relative to waves, to boats,
to wakes, or winds, but within their own immersions.
I watch until the heavy woman's friend is watching me
beneath her straw flower brim. I smile and turn
into the careful appraisal of the little girl's eyes,
a deeper bronze than her braids. It's all

that occurs, takes place, goes under,
these forever forms of water, and forms
that stride through them, dive in,
carelessly plunge,
carefully wade, how they
change, always
change.

## BENEATH ITS FLASHING SURFACE

A woman huddles, stares
at the space between her calves,
it becomes a sort of road
in its own geometry. An opening
to people walking by
her blanket by the pond.

The road has a vanishing point.
She follows it far enough
to notice a red-haired child
crying over too much now,
a grandmother who hobbles past
gives no comfort to the child,

her face is like a rusty leaf as
she mumbles there is enough gold
in Autumn left to mine. The child
continues to whimper as a crowd
of gnats cloud over the woman's head.
She pays attention to the cloud

as if it were a thought, as if
thoughts could be other lives
assembling themselves above
her upturned face. Schools of gnats
swim the sunset until she realizes
the old woman and child are gone.

Their absence is a despair.
The woman bends over the pond
to watch her face wavy on the surface.
Beneath its flashing surface
fish appear and disappear,

like thoughts.

## SHADES

Today's sky is unspeakably blue
in the heights of itself
but here, within my grasp,
it disappears.
Turpentined thumbs try
to push it oily
from thalo, from cerulean, indigo
onto white, into space, but
it moves away like the blaze
of today's sky or tomorrow's gray.

There are more layers of gray
to tomorrow's sky than doubts
in a absolute, than whites
in one chrysanthemum, more
than my eyes could mix
from cerebrated blacks or scribbled blues
on crowds of cloudy paper. I am
imagining

apparatus for distillation
of blazing blues. Sky
would bend around each elbow
of glass tubing, nudged
by its own pressures and
a considered flame, vaporizing
condensing, like cyanotic water.

My forehead seams
with shadows of sky-filtered space.
I press my thumbs against this crease,
my frown that lies
between blue fears

and gray consolations.

## HOLD THAT THOUGHT

so I hold it and
my arms ache with the pull,
the sensational chore
of holding one thought
while others stampede
around mind canyons,
kicking up dust, one must,
I understand, corral them.

So I corral them.
Stomping, snorting, maybe
mustangs, definitely wild,
hard to break or saddle.
These thoughts aren't tamable,
not with leads, or even
whispering, it seems there must
be some secret, but for now
split rails barely
contain them,

contain only those
I'm able to round up.
their nostrils flare, their eyes
wild and beautiful, so
out of control, and
what of all the others,
the herds
and herds,

thundering in the canyons
and valleys. This, a wild breed,
no Tennessee walkers or Morgans,
not the predictable brute strength

of a draft. Only mustangs,
matted manes, flying tails,
cutting hoof prints deep
into my dusty convolutions.

# BUT THEN

I bristled when
a writer called the sea
a great whore, but then
she breathes fish and waves
at anyone, never resisting
plunges, but sometimes coldly asking
death. Her salty depths

a still basic secret. This greatest part
of a world, a much painted lady,
slaps at any interruptions. She undermines
solid structures, sways
in brazen bitchiness for a sailor's love
or dread, she empties or fills
in changeable cycles, choosing

to contain life or wash it from her.
Water, not professing to be the oldest,
but then, it follows reason
her generous wetness
would have quenched even first
white-hot eruptions, shifting
with moon time, allowing
quickening in her tempered warmth.

## MAIDEN VOYAGE

A titan, designed
for dreams, for pausing on deck
to stare dream at rippling horizons,
or to play at shuffleboard
against a post card sky, or to lie
on a deck chair, sweetly bored.

Staterooms line like listed names
on separate levels, she noted hers,
and hummed along, pausing
at the deck railing to see
the iceberg, water wall
of frigid and some design.

It crashed its deafening cymbals
for the orchestrated ending of things
and torn steel shrieked, the titan
lurched, as churning sea
and panicked waves of people
gushed together over the sides.

She clawed for railing, grabbing only
thought - I haven't seen the entire ship-
the thought refrains rippled along
her mind's fading horizons
as she began, in fluted notes,
to breathe the sea.

## STANDARD SOURCES

Intending to inspire,
sombre cast-iron nuns
hammer martyrdom
into soft white-hot imaginations.
Impressions harden
and remain, stories
of martyrs for purity,
always women,

resisting the flesh,
always murdered intact.
Tales smoldering with passion
and innocence like St. Maria,
backing away from the gardener.
Impelled by seed, he came so close.
His scent was soil and blossoms
and how he raged at her refusals.

Maria's still chaste soul emerged
from one of fourteen
flooding incisions, opened
by his knife. And the serious nuns
go on to explain to all the waiting
widening eyes and ears how
a martyr for purity often appears
to her murderer, shining
soft forgiveness all around him,

he being only human… this
may be saintliness
but this is how
convention is forged,
by nuns or dogma,

how standards become
and remain
so black and white.

# ST. CROIX

Did I drown three times,
and were three times enough,
then surface and follow the waves
to these sandy edges, where now,
I hold reverent watch
as the sun places itself
before the flushed horizon?

One time before time,
rock and coral shuddered
pushed up from the sea,
greened itself with palms and cactus,
rain forest and hibiscus,
moved with geckos and flamboyant birds,
and finally,
brown children who smiled open

and watched with innocent eyes.
Did Christ want to swim off this very beach?
He would have easily laughed with the island,
while the people fished all the day,
and all night sent their love sighs
to follow the breezes all the way,
all the way to meet the emerging moon,
the stars pulling her up from her swim.

## SOLSTICE DREAM

Silhouetted by moon-filled window
the tree stands in garland and gleam,
in hushed Christmas repose until
wisps of smoke begin, drift
and lace around lower branches
until glitter is blurred and slowly,
blown-glass sheen is eclipsed
by thickening smoke, until
a wire sparks and an inner bough
becomes a flame.

Now, in the moon filled window,
a cone of fire, garland melting,
sap and resin snapping in the heat
until above the flames a white quilt
floats slowly down, drapes itself,
smothering the Christmas holocaust,
and after there is a need to blame,
the plug, the assembly of ornament,
the number of colored lights.

## ORNAMENT

Too much for an archangel,
this is a seraphim task
to catalog every color
that trickles among silver strands,
singing white, red, yellow, blue,
white, green, violet, white,
flashes and dazzle, an evergreen
in jewelry, miracles completed
in the eyes, sight, sight,
light for the solstice.

## SO BETWEEN

Trail goes along a mountain, you gestured
as cub master, indian guide, but I sighed,
half listening, staring at a rock
painted in large red strokes
God. *Graffiti*, you laughed. I laughed too.
This was a top of the world trail.

*There must have been a fire, something...*
you almost whispered, your voice oppressed,
as if something was sucked into empty sky
as we stared down into a burned out landscape.
My thoughts fell in red strokes, *It's like*
*we are survivors, after war, first exploring.*

I went closer to the edge. All those skeletal trees
pointing at the vast aluminum sky, an incinerated
mountainside plunging to join the other, rising green,
gridded with neighborhoods, factories humming,
puffing sky stains. *This is some view,* your voice soft.
I answered, *it's quiet, seems so between.*

Mute rocks and jagged stumps plummeting
to abruptly meet ascending life and the wind
did not explain. It whooshed by our ears
as two black hawks spiraled above us. *They glide*
*forever on air currents,* you were relieved
to explain something. I watch them circling
circling.

## LOVE POEM

The brook brightens
with its chance
to separate into sparkles,
caress each of your ankles,
and tumble on,
under willows and wind.

KATHLEEN MOSER

## FUR, FEATHERS, FELLOWSHIP

## WHEN JACKIE LEFT

When the vet recommended
putting him down, I remembered
setting a kitten on the linoleum,
telling the farmer we'd take him.
Weightless fur and bones, he was
a small tabby piece of the large light.

Thirteen years after his naming,
Jackie begins to darken,
not enough bright strength to purr.
In the animal hospital that night
Jackie decides on his own
before we are able to.

We bring him home.
He is cold heavy fur.
I stroke his empty body
as David digs as if angry at the dirt,
a hole never seems deep enough
next to the new hemlock tree.

We cry in the unreal dusk,
our faces gold in withdrawing light.
Rosy air moves behind the trees
over the cornfield,
over another death, over
the red plastic empty bowl.

## THE BO DOG

I have in mind something druid,
Merlin or Pendragon, or literary
like Argus, maybe Cerberus,
and he will be a 'blessed wolf'
like Jack London's Buck or White Fang.
But all my coddled pretensions whimper
and slink away, when Justin names him
(and it is his dog after all)
when Justin names him Bo.

Long faced puppy, cringes near the cat,
wags his tail hard against the wall
as food pours into his well chewed bowl.
He puppies around the house
for almost a week before I realize
this is no Cerberus, no regal wolf,
this is just Bo dog
who pukes in the car, gives rides
to hitchhiking fleas and ticks,
chews the Ikea catalog,

And magical bonds
with noble savage beasts
become just so much puppy chow, and now
Bo muddy paws my white shoes,
quivers a greeting, races
through the living room, cactus plants
across the oriental rug.  He sits
in the middle of his new Sahara,
sweeping potting soil back and forth,
in a happiness that fills
the whole of his doggy skull.

## MY GOOD DOG, MR. BO DOG,

has always been a generous soul, panting love in buckets
all over my lap while I scratch behind his floppy,
silky ears. He understands at levels to mystify
philosophers or scientists, and he's wise
like prophets and saints must be, but all humility
in his eagerness to love. Though too weak
to even drink water, he thumps his tail and
raises his head as I approach him. His body
fails him but his amazing soul, blazing
from sweetest eyes, connects hard with my soul,
behind my waterfall of tears. Believe this Bo.
I will hold your head the entire time. I will
hold onto you hard as you leave, as I promised,
no matter how it hurts, you won't be alone.

And so it does hurt, hurts beyond even my imaginings,
beyond any understanding I've held about pain.
We drive you home from the vet one last time.
Near your favorite white pine tree David digs
in July heat, and I grieve and grieve, walk and walk.
I vomit grief, sob grief, grief pounds behind my eyes.
I wander our emptier home, looking for my dog,
asking you to come, needing to rub your head,
feel your paws, snuggle into your fur, just one more time,
to lie next to you on the living room rug and whisper,
as I always did, many times every day, since the day
a long-nosed, round-bellied pup came home with us,
only your short, blessed lifetime ago, just once more, to whisper
into your silky ear as you squirm and grunt with delight...
*you are the best, Bo, the best of all the doggies*
*in the whole and entire universe.*

## THE FAOLIN PAGE

Little long nose, get to know me,
for you see, I've known so deeply
one of your kind. A dog soul
so wide-open to mine,
that we spoke with just our eyes.
But he had to leave his old fur place,
his doggy skull and happy tail,
and I struggled to find the will
to want another dog. Now,
here you are little wolf one,
groaning against my hugs,
love nibbling along my arm and I wonder
how wide our bridge will grow to be,
your heart to my heart, my soul
to yours. When your doggy thoughts
begin to move in harmonics
with my tenacious child dreams,
we will be easy together, but
however our bridge builds itself,
it will be ours, so Faolin little wolf,
welcome to the pack.

## AS FAR AS REX CAN KNOW

(for our Tabby cat named for dinosaurs)

divinity walks on two legs,
makes sounds and pictures
from a box, provides food
endlessly, makes fire at will
moves away every morning
inside rumbling worlds and returns
in rumbling worlds each night,
makes much more conversation
than what's between a growling
and a purr, provides comfort,
with a stroke and
permits all cat
existence.

## STILL

I can feel sunlight
hot on Faolin's fur, watch it play
as sunlight adores to do,
through tangles of locust leaves,
pirouetting prettily down, all the way
to ground cover, jeweling the ivy
and switching on daffodils.
I still can see sunlight
gilding the rims of three drifted clouds
just to the left of tall swaying oaks
and waving hemlocks, sunlight
pouring its glare along the spoutings
and brazenly baking driveway macadam
into a ribbon of steam after rain.
Still there remains sunlight
a smirking of shine
on the hummingbird feeder
reminding how shine
will always return after
lightning and thunder
slam their doors to leave.
Still there will be again
and again, sunlight
on the compost pile, Douglas firs,
golden delicious apple blossoms,
greener than ever winter wheat,
lilacs and honeysuckle, dogwood and rose,
effortless sunlight
on the endless world.

## GREEN EYED ENVY

He's a funny comfort
a rumbling wearing fur,
this pressure on my belly,
his eyes to slits and rhythmic purr,
the plain ecstatic catness of him.
I know it's never been
snaked into his feline mind
to hate himself, to want to end,
to puzzle over any meaning
in becoming and continuing as cat.

It maybe isn't that I am jealous
of my tabby cat, but rather
the simplicity of cat thought or
the complexity
of his purring breathing waves
of I am I am I am I am.

# FINBAR RILEY

To Finbar
it is understated redundancy
to say he is
an exquisite cat.
He blinks. His eyes,
smoldering gold,
gaze back at me
because
he can so easily see
his value in my eyes
and, when combined
with the inherent self esteem
given to all cats, it becomes
almost insufferable,
were it not that
I love my cat.

## CAMOUFLAGE

I'm only sitting here,
only watching
carp.

I have to harp
on insufficient camouflage,
some silver browns
there, spectral and
barely seen, have
fishy discretion.
But that one glowing
blatantly orange, a dayglo
swish of tail, I saw
immediately, more
obvious.

I'm only sitting
here, only
watching.

## MONSIGNOR MANTIS

Mantis preying
posing mechanical
on a knobby twig,
mandibles moving,
devoutly snatching
chewing, reverently
grinding life
to buzzless juices,
swallowed into
hallowed places,
praying
mantis
monster face,
unblinking faceted eyes.

## BICYCLING AT DUSK

and grabbing my breaths
in rhythmic gasps,
I inhale a swarm of gnats
like dirty air,
pesting lives
gathering in sky,
only to be caught
in mucous or
sneezed
back into evening.

## DROUGHT

It had been weeks without rain.
Days stacked themselves
nothing flowed.
Sunday I watched birds
sit without moving
on window sills
on other waiting places.
Wednesday they hid their heads
under dusty wings.
Thursday arrives dressed dazzling
in pewter and haze
until the sky is persuaded
to unlace her billowed gray blouse...
late afternoon weeps with relief,
with so much rain.

From the balcony,
with mist against my eyes,
I watch five birds play so high
in timeless clouds, higher
than I thought birds are able
to fly.
Five black beating dreams climbing
platinum sky in all the rain.
Two pause, shake their wings,
one loops. All five dip and whirl
in celebration of rain.
They are alive
in our tumbling wet world
where life is so in love
with water.

## THAT BIRD

steps
uncertain,
placing bird claw
over bird claw
carefully,
as if
each weightless step
has impact,
as if
its odd
pas d' oiseau
might cause
such bird
reverberations.

## WINTER EARLY

Those rising bird shapes
behind icy roofs,
this gray gasp behind my teeth.

## EXISTENTIAL

It is not my reality
to be red,
complained an apple,
blushing.
I will ripen, but
not redden and
certainly not fall.
...discretely, by the stem,
luminous tiny thought worm
curly twisted a dream
toward her core,
curly twisted...

still the apple,
daily more the same,
finally bore her name
red delicious to the ground,
to be eaten
by the highest
and lowest
shapes of life.

## IT WAS A DEER

She does not appear.
We feel the deer, a sudden
deafening impact
against the driver's side,
a blur of brown. Now,
she lies in the middle of the road.
She raises her head, two times
and again. She struggles.
Her pain and terror seem
to burn inside my own mind.
Her large ears twitch, her body shudders.
I hold my tears because Hannah
is six years old and so afraid.
*We must stay in the car Hannah.*
*Pappy will be back soon.* David
runs to help slow other cars
approaching the dying,
exquisite deer in the road.
She is moments from death,
I am a longer time away. Someone
asks about a gun. One man brings a knife.
Two others hold her head with her ears.
It's too slow, too cold. I strain toward
her wild spirit as it leaves
for somewhere. I finally cry
alone, in bed,
with my blackened dreams.

## SEAL COATS

Men
about their business
club and skin babies.

Twitching shiny bodies
shudder naked into death
staining these frosty altars
so blazing Arctic white
a deep and spreading red.

It's this expensive,
soft white skins of innocence
that we pull around our shivering
absence of fur.

## THE DOGS

The times my eyes
scream in this dream.
I try not to watch
the boy stumble.
It keeps replaying, rewinding,
until he staggers and dies
before ridiculous doctors
marking data, how many times
they had broken his skull.

The times my heart
shudders in this dream,
Exploding black shepherd
lunges, strains against his chain,
his gnashing teeth flash
like the blessed links and
I can't run. I'm a child
before a vicious dog,
under a wrong star.

The times my mind
cries in this dream.
Trees hold their breath,
no joy, air or light,
just one ghost white shepherd,
slinking with dark wet eyes.
He whimpers and whines
as though I should
stroke his doggy skull,
as though I should, but
I walk away

into paths of florescent azaleas

and blossoming trees that pant perfume,
and my dream tumbles, tumbles.

## EVE OF JULY

For the eve of July, it is unusually cold
at a party in a back yard in upstate New York.
Welcome and arrivals twilight long tables
of vodka and wine and Russian magic of cabbage.
Two Ukrainian stars whose faces shine
all dimensions of smile in stark relief
of the American porch light. A friend's foreign home
and an audience eager for the promise of music.
It is a gift. We don't know how to thank.

And the gratitude of a bear on a Pennsylvania highway,
whose fur gleamed like black night at noon,
galloping four lanes, a width of rapid dangers.
Brake lights alarmed with their sudden reds.
Everyone slowed, seemed glad he had made it
from green to green, this clumsy man from other worlds,
tree worlds. I pressed my pedal again and nudged
the volume of my Russian composers louder.

Sweet vocal symphony from across the world,
their voices gusty into cold summer air,
this fairy tale pair singing Russian lyrics
to those who stand so still to listen.
Later, we drink more vodka and wine,
eat halupkis, wonderful black bread, and
I remember my bear, how we slowed
everything down and how he had made it.
For the eve of July, we should feel warm.

# ABOUT THE AUTHOR

Kathleen Moser completed her degrees in Art and English at SUNY Brockport, NY. She attended writers conferences in Brockport, NY, Squaw Valley CA, and in New Hampshire where she worked with William Heyen, Stanley Plumly, Galway Kinnell and Sharon Olds, among others. She has never stopped writing.

Kathleen Moser lives in New Tripoli, Pennsylvania with her husband. She spent years working as a medical editor, raising two children, and recovering from childhood abuse. Much of her early successes in publication were in poetry journals until she had to withdraw from all of that to deal with flashbacks and healing. After much encouragement from her husband, she decided to put these books out in the world. She and her husband David have 3 grandchildren. Life is a blessing.

www.ingramcontent.com/pod-product-compliance
Lightning Source LLC
LaVergne TN
LVHW050336160826
845677LV00014B/3637

*9798837998928*